Get your **FREE** gift
to make reading even
more entertaining and fun!

Follow the link via QR-code:

ttps://aw18ab9b.aweb.page/p/2f9c0917-d5f0-47b3-b3d1-611ffa84659a

or simply send us an email on
goodzilla.books@gmail.com

You are more than welcome
to leave a review on our Amazon page!

The sun woke up and spread its charm.
There is ONE sleepy house on ONE sleepy farm.

ONE cat climbs and runs on the roof.
TWO dogs are barking loudly, "Woof!"

THREE cows are chewing tasty and crispy hay.
TWO mice are playing on this sunny day.

Cock-a-doodle-doo!
ONE rooster is happy and cheerful, as well.
FOUR horses run across the green field and dell.

FOUR yellow chickens came out of their eggs.
FIVE hens watch them peck between their legs.

FIVE birds sing on the branches of ONE tree.
SIX apples are as red and yummy as they can be.

SEVEN cute rabbits are ready for the first bite.
FOUR of them are gray, and THREE of them are white.

And down in the pigsty, **EIGHT** piglets are calm.
FIVE of them drink milk from **ONE** caring mom.

Out of nowhere,
   the poultry broke the morning peace.
Splashing water all around,
   SIX ducks joined NINE geese.

Not so far from here, **TEN** sheep graze white as a cloud.
"Woof-woof! Don't get lost!" TWO guard dogs bark aloud.

Now everyone is awake and ready to play.
How many different animals do you see on this day?

Thank you for reading this book!

Did you enjoy it?

Please, share your honest review on Amazon.

(Honestly, that's the only legal way to get better ranks on Amazon)

GOODZILLA BOOKS

Made in the USA
Coppell, TX
05 November 2021